I0450600

Validation Denied
Grace Bestowed

Validation Denied
Grace Bestowed

◆

*somewhere between the
ghetto and God
was something called
foster care...*

Quelyn Purdie

iUniverse, Inc.
New York Lincoln Shanghai

Validation Denied Grace Bestowed
somewhere between the
ghetto and God
was something called
foster care...

All Rights Reserved © 2004 by Quelyn Purdie

No part of this book may be reproduced or transmitted in any form or by any means, graphic, electronic, or mechanical, including photocopying, recording, taping, or by any information storage retrieval system, without the written permission of the publisher.

iUniverse, Inc.

For information address:
iUniverse, Inc.
2021 Pine Lake Road, Suite 100
Lincoln, NE 68512
www.iuniverse.com

Back Cover Photo by: Michael Scott Jones, www.msjimages.com

ISBN: 0-595-32477-0 (pbk)
ISBN: 0-595-66596-9 (cloth)

Printed in the United States of America

I offer this work to the Lord,
The One who guides my hand and pen

To Ma and Dad
For your relentless care and love for me
since age 9.

Contents

AUTHOR'S NOTE

I began to write *Validation Denied, Grace Bestowed* in 1996. As I wrote, I wondered if I could remember enough material for a book. I was fascinated by how clips from a past I had completely forgotten effortlessly appeared in my mind's eye. I was even more surprised when I did not feel any residual sadness, resentment or even contentment as I wrote this story (I believe that this is due to years of personal growth through self-improvement seminars and spirituality that helped me to heal. Although making progress was no "walk in the park", the freedom I experienced at every turn was as though someone lifted one-thousand pounds off my chest, and I could breathe once again). I was more concerned about writing the truth as clearly, yet as creatively as possible for you, the public.

I discovered that this book *had* to be written, for one, *Validation Denied, Grace Bestowed* is, for me, a huge expression of gratitude for the people and events that led me to realize that grace had been present all along; and two, I see the book as a profound possibility to help others, especially youth living in foster care, to courageously and coherently shed light on their own experience and to move forward with a greater sense of peace, joy, and integrity.

There are details of my past I simply do not remember, therefore, *Validation Denied, Grace Bestowed* is written to the best of my recollection. Furthermore, the surnames of those other than family have been omitted to protect their privacy.

Peace.

SNAPSHOT: An Introduction

The following is a narrative excerpted from a screenplay I wrote. The narrative is an example of how children are "removed" from their home due to neglect or abuse:

Carlita, 19 and pregnant, rubs her belly as she pours cereal into three bowls. She waddles toward the refrigerator, opens the door and searches for milk but there is none. Frustrated, she quickly waddles into her bedroom, grabs keys and purse and returns to the living room where her siblings, Felicia, 14, and brothers Carlos and Ralphie, 6 and 8 respectively, are watching TV.

"I'm going to the store. I'll be right back. Felicia you're in charge."

"When's Ma coming home?"

"I don't know, but Daddy should be walking in any minute now. Clean up and prepare his bath water. He's been on the road day and night for the past couple of days."

As soon as Carlita leaves, Ralphie pops Carlos on the head and Carlos chases Ralphie. Felicia yells at the boys as she tidies up the living room.

"Carlos and Ralphie, sit down. Now! I'm going to take a shower so don't open the door for no one except Daddy, Carlita or Ma and don't mess up the living room again."

The boys behave until Felicia enters the bathroom, shuts the door and turns on the shower. The boys continue to roughhouse.

At a corner bodega, Carlita grabs a carton of milk and proceeds down the aisle toward the cashier. A hooded person busts into the store, points a gun at the cashier and demands cash. Carlita freezes, unnoticed.

The cashier quickly pulls out a gun hidden under the drawer and shoots at the burglar. A shootout begins as Carlita inches toward the exit, but just before she dashes out, she is hit in the back by a stray bullet. She falls. The burglar runs out of the bodega, stepping over Carlita's body. The cashier emerges from behind the counter holding the side of his head with a blood-drenched wad of paper towel.

Carlita gasps for life as she lies in a pool of blood. The cashier grabs his phone and dials 911.

Carlos pitches a plastic baseball to Ralphie who swings, hitting the ball against a wall in the living room. A picture falls and the boys wince.

Felicia yells at the boys from the bathroom. "Carlos and Ralphie, sit down!"

"We are sitting down!" Carlos chases Ralphie around furniture marked as "bases." The doorbell rings.

Ralphie stops running and Carlos plops on top of him, out of breath. They look at one another. Ralphie stammers, "Who is it?"

"Ralphie? Open the door, Poppy."

"Where's your key?"

"Oh, Poppy, you know Mommy forgets sometimes. C'mon Baby, open the door, Mommy's got to pee."

Ralphie jumps up and opens the door. A woman social worker and a cop walk into the apartment. Carlos starts to cry. The cop asks Ralphie, "Do you know where your parents are, Son?" Ralphie yells, "Felicia! They're going to take us! Felicia!"

The cop and social worker glance at one another. Felicia slips out of the bathroom and into her bedroom, unnoticed.

The cop searches the apartment for Felicia who is already climbing out of the window in her bathrobe and sneakers. She is clutching a track trophy. The cop busts into her room. Felicia glares at the cop and disappears. The cop rushes toward the window. Felicia jumps from the bottom rung of a fire escape ladder and lands safely onto the sidewalk. The cop calls for backup.

Another cop car skids around the street corner. Felicia sprints in the opposite direction with the car gaining on her but she disappears in a crowd of pedestrians.

Carlita dies on the operating table at a hospital.

Carlos and Ralphie cry as they leave the apartment with the social worker and policeman.

—Adapted from screenplay, *Glenda's Girls*

When authorized individuals show up, oftentimes unannounced, to get the children wherever they may be—usually at home, school, emergency center or hospital, it's called a "removal" in social work terms. I learned this during fifteen years of working with youth. As an educator, I have worked as a public school teacher, tutor and I have taught at The Bridges Juvenile Center (formerly known as Spofford Juvenile Detention) in Bronx, New York. I have also performed casework at an independent living program for teenagers in foster care.

Oftentimes the parents are not present when children are removed, as it was with Ralphie and Carlos….and my brother, J.P. and me.

We were removed from Jacqueline's care, unbeknownst to her. We had been left alone again, for the second day in a row. I later learned that Jacqueline was a drug addict.

We were bounced from home to home amongst relatives who, it seems, shielded us from the pain and revolution of the sixties. I didn't get the chance to march or raise my little fist and holler the words "Black power!" and I didn't feel any emotion when Rev. Dr. Martin Luther King, Jr., President John F. Kennedy and Malcolm X were assassinated.

I was fine, as long as I was with family, especially Daddy. I did not know my father until I was about six when he and my grandmother got J.P. and me from a shelter, where we were "placed" after the cops "removed" us from Jacqueline's apartment.

I was Daddy's little girl, his princess. He made me feel like a queen. Then one day, I was dethroned. I became a "foster" child (as if I needed *another* label by which society could define me and act accordingly).

I felt that I had to defend myself against my new label so I "acted out" but not to the point where I'd jeopardize any possibility of returning to Daddy or any other relative, for that matter. So, I didn't steal, beat up anyone, destroy the homes I lived in nor was I verbally abusive, promiscuous or incarcerated. I did, however, have a nasty attitude, especially when I was angry or moody. I missed my father—only he could restore his little princess to her rightful place at his side by coming back to reclaim her. There was a ray of hope when Daddy visited me in the foster home and promised he'd return.

When I went away to college, my attitude, mood swings and need for validation magnified. Sometimes I felt satisfied, but it was often at the expense of others' feelings and my own integrity. All this would translate into a bittersweet young adult life until I was invited to a most auspicious event that would alter my life. Through the prescribed spiritual practices of meditation, prayer, selfless service and self-inquiry I discovered that grace was present all along and that my quest for personal validation was really a journey toward Self-reconciliation—but I had to carry a shovel along the way....

Removed

We lived in a small two-bedroom, roach-infested apartment in Brooklyn, maybe Flatbush or Bedstuy. It was normal for J.P. and me, four and six, to eat starch right out of the blue and white box as though we were eating potato chips. About two or three days a week Jacqueline would leave us alone until the next morning or night. The most painful part of this was having to answer my brother's question, "When is mommy coming home?" "Soon" or "Don't worry, she'll be back", I answered as I stared out of our kitchen window.

Jackie did not physically abuse me but one day she did scare the hell out of me. Before she left the house in the morning, she told me to have our room clean and laundry sorted before she returned. When Jackie returned at night, and high, I had not done what I was told. She went to the kitchen and returned to our room with a sardonic grin on her face and a knife. She grabbed my right wrist and mockingly traced circles around it threatening to cut it off. From then on our room was as spotless as I could get it.

Jackie had a boyfriend named Alex who would visit, have sex with her then exit. My mother must have loved or cared for him enough, though, to dash out of the house one summer evening with J.P. and me, jump into a cab, and race toward the hospital. Alex had been shot. I felt frightened but not remorseful since I really did not know Alex. I only knew that they often fought, had sex, got high and then exited.

One day in the summer, J.P. and I were home playing with our toys. I loved my brother dearly. We rarely fought and whatever we did together, we had a ball. J.P. would have me rolling because he was good at imitating people. I always felt that he should have become a stand-up comedian, or since he could swim like a fish, become an Olympic swimmer. Instead, after he graduated high school, he chose to enroll in the Army. J.P. always liked martial arts and anything else that disciplined the body.

Our neighbor across the hall asked me where my mother was. Of course I did not know. Shortly after my neighbor's inquisition, there was a firm knock on our apartment door. "Who is it?" I cheerfully asked, hoping it was Jacqueline. It was the police. I touched the doorknob to the protest of my brother who reminded me: "Ma said not to open the door for NO body!" "It's the police," I pleaded.

The police instructed me to put on a dress my mother had laid out the night before. She always did that before she "went out." My brother was to put on some pants. I asked the policemen if we could bring some of our toys, and they conceded. I remember feeling both sad and relieved. We cooperated with no fight, just my brother's tears and fear on his face.

I wanted to see you, run to you
and shout, "Mommy!" or "Mom!" one day
which never came.
I wanted to show the world that
I have (my own) mom, who I would treat like a
Queen, and who would train me to be the same.
But, this was validation denied.
It's been a while now, Mother

and I was embraced by strangers
who gave me a resting place.
Maybe
you are now someone else's mom
(do they resemble my face?)
If this is true, Mother
you have my wish for happiness.
If it is not so,
you have my wish for happiness.
Past no longer owns me.

Time canceled all my pain.
Grace colored my tears sun rain
and Life
is now my garden of purpose and love.
Mother, for you, I wish the same.
                    —From *Sacred Blues, Poetry*

The police drove us to a children's shelter where we remained for about a month during the summer until our grandmother and father came for us. I never knew who my father was until then. I only knew about Alex, Jacqueline's boyfriend.

"Who's *that?*" I was always the curious type, unafraid to inquire about things. My grandmother seemed a little surprised, but she introduced the handsome, deep-complexion, medium-height man, beaming at me by saying, "That's your Daddy." "My *real* Daddy?" They laughed as my father hugged and squeezed me. We smiled at one another as though we were just married. I could finally utter the word, "daddy." He spoke politely to J.P. who wanted a hug too. I could tell. His body craved it, but to no avail, even though he was named after my father. Even now, J.P. refuses to be called his full name.

Shirley

Daddy took J.P. and me to Shirley's place, a two or three-bedroom apartment where he introduced us to Shirley and her son, Kenneth. I think Shirley was Daddy's girlfriend. She was tall, had a beautiful deep complexion, and a great body. I remember desiring long, shapely legs like Shirley's. She wore glasses like I did, and she always kept herself well-groomed.

Kenneth was taller and a little older than me. We got along for the most part but Kenneth was sort of a mischievous nerd. Sometimes he was generous with his board games and other times he'd be selfish, when noone was looking. I didn't like playing with dolls, so I'd play with Kenneth's GI Joes and racecar set complete with tracks, a remote control and accessories.

Daddy disciplined Kenneth like the rest of us, although he was softer on me. Shirley was actively involved in our education. I remember walks to the library where I got my first library card. Shirley also helped us with our homework and encouraged us to watch educational TV shows like *The Mickey Mouse Club, Mr. Roger,* and *Romper Room.* "See me walk so straight and tall…," Shirley would echo when I didn't walk or sit erect. We also played board games like Monopoly and Checkers. I still enjoy board games. My favorite game is chess, even though you'd probably beat me within the first couple of moves.

There were a few things I did not like about Shirley. I hated it when she'd make oatmeal for breakfast and okra for dinner. She would give me a very small portion of okra so all I had to do was hold my nose and quickly stuff the slimy vegetable into my mouth. I couldn't do that with oatmeal. She knew I didn't like it (I couldn't digest the milk she used as an ingredient. I didn't know that back then) and she'd give me too much. One morning, Shirley made oatmeal. She plopped a smaller portion in my bowl and told me to have it finished before she returned to the kitchen to wash the dishes. So, I took a few swallows and in about five seconds it splattered back into the bowl.

Kenneth said "Eeeeewww!" loud enough so that Shirley and Daddy could hear him. Before I could get rid of the evidence, Shirley stormed into the kitchen. She asked what had happened, and, of course, Kenneth was more than happy to report the news. Shirley commanded me to eat the oatmeal-vomit. I looked at her as though she had three heads, but before long, she smashed the whole damn bowl of oatmeal-vomit into my face. This is probably why I don't laugh when I see people on TV get a pie in the face. I cried and I was so angry I wanted to shoot her. Daddy just stood by watching, feeling sorry for me.

One day when he was holding my hand during one of our (cherished) outings, I asked Daddy why I had to eat oatmeal since I did not like it. Daddy said, "Because it's good for you," and that if I liked hanging out with him, which truly was the epitome of my existence, I *had* to eat my oatmeal. My first thought was that maybe he was scared of Shirley, after all, she did seem to be the dominant one in the home. Perhaps Daddy was a "playah," jumping from one woman's house to the next. Anyhow, I psyched myself out and my stomach to love the beige-colored glob. Today, I love oatmeal, but I don't use dairy—only rice milk. As for okra, I love it now, especially as gumbo.

Living with Shirley ultimately made me feel anxious. I began to pick my hair and my fingers, especially my thumbs. I would pick my thumbs bloody. Shirley would harass me about not picking my hair and thumbs and Daddy would try to get me to stop so that she would stop harassing me. But when I was alone with Daddy, I never picked my hair and fingers.

One day Daddy asked me if I wanted to meet my cousins. He had a way of asking me if I wanted to do something that made me feel as though I was going to meet God in person. And no matter what we ended up doing, I had a good time with my father. So I was thrilled to know that I had more folks I would know as family and could hang with. When we got to the house, there was a room filled with beautiful people eating, drinking, playing cards, dancing and laughing. Daddy proudly introduced me to the people. He loved showing me off, and I loved the attention. I'm not certain if my relatives were mostly from my father's side, but I didn't care. They were my relatives. A James Brown record came on and Daddy invited me to dance with him, to everyone's delight. All of us partied all night.

Today, I wouldn't recognize anyone, except Daddy and J.P. If anyone were to walk up to me and say they are a cousin or an aunt, I'd have to ask for proof.

Daddy and Grandma

Daddy was a business administrator who would show off his little girl to his colleagues and friends. I felt pretty when I was with my father. He'd have Shirley dress me in a cute shorts set or a dress, patent leather shoes and ankle socks when we were going 'bye-bye'. Daddy was my king.

When my days seem dark as night, Daddy
and my spirit is low
I think of all the good times we had
and night becomes a rainbow!

when Ma went away
I had no doubt that you could abundantly
educate, feed me or quench my thirst

you taught me how to be a lady
you taught me how to drive
you said never act shady
and you taught me how to strive
when my days seem dark as night, Daddy
and my spirit is low
I think of all the good times we had
and night becomes a rainbow!

when I gave into temptation and did wrong
you taught me how to be strong
when I was choosing the wrong kind of fella
you always said, "Princess! You can do even better!"

I will die loving you, I will die loving you
when my days seem dark as night
and my spirit is low
I think of all the good times we had
and night becomes a rainbow!

I think of all the good times we had Daddy
and night becomes a rainbow!
　　　　　　—"A Father's Day Song" adapted from *Sacred Blues Poetry*

I loved Daddy, but he never acknowledged or fully accepted my brother as his son. "Because he doesn't look like me," he said to me one day when I asked. I was stunned and hurt, and when J.P. revealed how Daddy would beat and punish him for seemingly trivial reasons, my heart ached. Sometimes Daddy wouldn't let J.P. play with me. I couldn't stand it because J.P. was my best friend. Perhaps we were sister and brother by different women but I didn't care, J.P. was my brother. Besides, I had wondered where Daddy was when the cops came to get us.

Grandma had a beautiful brownstone in Brooklyn. I loved Brooklyn and still do. I loved being with Grandma. First of all, I lived like a queen. I slept in a queen-size bed in an elegantly designed and sweet-smelling master bedroom, all for myself. Grandma had a beautiful garden of flowers and vegetables in the backyard of her brownstone where J. P. and I were allowed to *carefully* play. We shared a red tricycle that we could ride on the short sidewalk around Grandma's garden. (And it wasn't about "accidentally" rolling the tricycle into the garden, either.) J.P. got more spankings than I did, but I don't remember Grandma being as discriminatory towards J.P. as Daddy. She was a disciplinarian. When we misbehaved we got the ironing cord, and back then that was not considered child abuse. And, we never felt abused.

Grandma made sure I was always healthy and that I learned and completed my assignments for school. The only thing I didn't like was the morning ritual of having a tablespoon of cod liver oil jammed into my mouth, and smelling like fish at least until midday. But, I was never *ever* ill—until I lived in foster care. Grandma made sure we looked good, especially for church. I wore black patent leather shoes, tights or cute white ankle socks, a skirt and blouse or a dress, a hat and white gloves. I liked church especially the singing, fellowship, and Grandma's mouthwatering Sunday meals.

Validation Denied

J.P. was with us only for a very short while. I do not remember how long, perhaps a month. Then, without warning or even a goodbye, J.P. was taken away by a social worker. No, he was snatched right from under my nose. I remember experiencing a quick pulsing sensation in the pit of my stomach, and then empty space. It was as though someone pulled the plug and all the electricity in my body drained out of me. Validation denied.

I was upstairs playing when Grandma called me downstairs to the kitchen. Daddy was there, looking sad. I knew this time he wasn't going to say something to make me feel as though I'd be meeting God in person. Daddy gingerly sat me on his lap. I thought what he was about to say had something to do with Grandma, but definitely not me. Basically, he said that Grandma was ill and could not take care of me anymore, and that I would stay with "someone else" until he could come for me. My face looked like a reflection of his, although there were no tears. I guess I was too shocked to be emotional at the time.

Within days, if not the next day, my grandmother was helping me pack while a professional-looking lady patiently waited. I asked Grandma why I *had* to go and she only repeated what my father said—that she was sick and couldn't take care of me anymore, but that I would see her again, soon. As I walked out the door, hand in hand with the lady, I looked back at my grandmother leaning on a chair by the kitchen table. She could barely lift her hand to wave goodbye. Daddy had already disappeared.

I don't remember if we took a cab or drove or took the subway to the agency but on the way there the lady, who I learned was a social worker, was sickeningly cheerful and pleasant. I guess she was trying to help me drown out the loud, eerie, clank of another broken chain in my heart.

The day seemed to go by quickly, as the worker kept me entertained and fed until they found a place for me. That evening I was driven in a nice car, by another worker, to Amityville, Long Island. I was anxious to see my new caretakers, and amazed at the spaciousness of Amityville which means The Friendly Village, as we drove through the small town and turned onto Jefferson Avenue.

The Johnson's

I was placed with the Johnson's. J.P. joined me about a month later. The Johnson's were a complete family. Foster care agencies try to place children in a two-parent home, preferably a married couple, like Mr. and Mrs. Johnson. They had two adopted children, Sylvia and Billy, who were about the same age as J.P. and I.

The Johnson's were a lot of fun and they were very caring, church-going people. We were only able to play in the yard or right in front of the gate within eyeshot of Mr. and Mrs. Johnson. Once in a while, we could visit a neighbor, either right next door or just across the street. Now that I have experience as a foster care worker, I can understand why my foster parents watched us like hawks. They had to take extra precaution because for one, we were young children, and two, we were not their own children so if anything serious happened to my brother and me, the Johnson's could possibly lose certification and be "closed." In other words, the Johnson's would no longer be able to give foster care.

Whenever Mr. and Mrs. Johnson went out or away for a short while they would send all of us down the street and around the corner on Campbell Street, to an incredible God-loving woman named Ms. Thomas. Ms. Thomas had been highly recommended for her relentless care and love for her own children and others.

I remember always feeling safe around Ms. Thomas who had incredible wit. You could not and would not pull the wool over her eyes. She would "check you" in a minute. Sometimes, if we'd stay the whole weekend, we were required to attend church with Ms. Thomas. If we were at her home during the week, she would make sure we completed our homework and give us menial chores to help her around the house. "Kwah-lyn", she'd call me. Although I was still in elementary school, Ms. Thomas would let me baby-sit her beautiful toddler when she went to the store. The boy had either been adopted or, as usual, Ms. Thomas opened her arms to care for him as a foster child. Somehow, in my heart I hoped the baby would stay with Ms. Thomas until he was old enough to be on his own. He deserved her love and care. And Ms. Thomas made you feel deserving.

When I lived with the Johnson's I developed a rare eye disease. I thought, 'What the hell is *this*?' I had previously enjoyed good health when I lived with my grandmother and now I have a *disease*. Not a simple illness where I'd just need a pill then be fine, but a disease! Before I became a vegetarian years later, I used to view disease as a permanent illness of the body. Irisitis. I had no conscious control over "Iris" and I am sure it was related to the shock of separation from my biological family. Oftentimes, depending on the child's age at the time of separation or removal from their biological family, the child experiences illnesses he or she never had before placement.

Anyhow, "Iris" affected one eye or the other, usually the right one, which would turn red and I'd experience migraine-like headaches. I would also desire sleep no matter the time of day, and I couldn't stand bright lights or sunlight.

One year I was in such pain, it nearly drove me insane. People thought I was crazy. I was hospitalized (in a regular hospital) and finally, someone from my own family showed up—Grandma. But I couldn't enjoy her company because I had just awakened, my eye hurt really bad and I felt drugged. I do remember Grandma placing something under my pillow, maybe a small Bible or spiritual quote. Eventually I got well enough to go home, but "Iris" would soon return and not go away until college.

After about a year or so, the Johnson's decided to move south. I felt I had been the one to drive them away. 'It was all "Iris's" fault', I'd think. However, the way the Johnson's broke the news to J.P. and me was acceptable. All of us took a short trip to an orchard or some kind of farm, further out on Long Island. When we returned home they sat us down and told us about their plans. I remember asking if Sylvia and Billy were going too and the answer was affirmative but that before J.P. and I moved to another home, Sylvia and Billy would be available to say their final goodbyes.

The Johnson's kept their word. And I was cool with that. To this day, keeping your word is paramount in maintaining my trust and friendship with you. Even if you need to break your word, tell me. Say *something*. Don't just leave me hanging. I believe that this is a major reason why so many relationships fail—business relationships, intimate relationships, friendships, and especially family.

Anyhow, the Johnson's bid us farewell as our social worker drove J.P. and me to another foster home just down the street.

The Vaughan's

Mr. Vaughan was an airline passenger screener for TWA and Mrs. Vaughan was the head teacher of a Head Start program not far from their home on Jefferson Avenue. Will, their son, is about my age. Then there's Valarie who has two gorgeous young adult men, and Joanne, who is single.

Valarie and Joanne are older than me and I saw them as my big sisters who could show me a thing or two about womanhood. I would observe and try to internalize Joanne's New York City wit and blend this cool way of being with Valarie's outspoken yet feminine demeanor. It didn't work. As a teenager I turned out to be a corny-dry-sense-of humor-moody-bookworm, contrary to J.P. who was the cool one and easier to be around. All of the Vaughan siblings were geniuses and are thriving today.

In the 70's I had some of the best times of my life because of the people, places and things the Vaughan's exposed J.P. and me to. There were family cookouts and parties in our huge, neatly trimmed, grassy backyard, and trips to other states (with the agency's permission). We visited California, New Mexico, Virginia, and Florida. In one of the cities, we saw the Four Tops at a hotel show. Today, they still look and sound fabulous.

I remember my first plane ride. We were going to either California or Albuquerque and I was afraid and in awe at the same time as I peeked out of my window and experienced the perfection and vastness of the sky.

Then came one of the most exciting days of my life. Ma surprised me one day with tickets to see The Jackson Five at the Westbury Music Fair. The day of the concert, Ma made an appointment with our hairdresser and I got all dolled up.

Valarie drove Will, J.P. and me to the concert which featured the one and only Janet Jackson. She was about five or six then, and she did her adorable impersonation of Mae West's "Hey there, lover boy!" It took about a month for me to digest the fact that I had gone to my first live concert and had seen my favorite group. More than two decades later, I would stand face to face with Janet (more on that later).

The 70's. I used to think Pam Grier's *Coffy* and *Foxy Brown* were the baddest women on the planet. And *Superfly* and *Shaft* were my kings. I guess they replaced Daddy, at least for the duration of the movie.

Drive-bys were unheard of in my neighborhood. We were preoccupied with boom boxes. The people with the biggest, boomingest box were the ones to hang with, especially if they had a car, Old English and some weed. I remember the mood rings. Pretty, colorful rings that changed colors according to your body heat. I was afraid to wear one because I thought it would always turn black and stay that way no matter how much I acted like things were cool—like the blue-light basement parties. Basements were transformed into sweatboxes as DJ's and MC's spinned the 'wheels of steel' and when they said to "throw your hands in the air and wave'em like ya just don't care", you gladly heeded the call. We'd almost dance a hole in the floor doing The Hustle, The Bump, The Freak, and freestyle to beats like *My Adidas*, *Cold Sweat*, *Freak Out*, *Rock The Bells*, and *Tear The Roof Off*. The DJ's and MC's performed some of the smoothest scratchin' and mixin' and Rap and Rhyme you rarely hear today.

In the summertime, there was a block party or community fair almost every other week. Sometimes radio personalities like the one and only late Frankie Crocker from WBLS, would host the fair where up and coming groups could showcase their talent.

I learned how to make simple meals even though one day I boiled an egg so hard the egg whites burst through the shell. I also learned how to vacuum and clean house using "elbow grease" as Ma would say. But when I learned how to ride a bike, with the help of neighborhood friends, I was elated because I could jump on my bike and go as far as my legs would take me, as long as I was home in time for dinner or before dusk. My first bike was bought "hot". When I started working at fourteen, I got myself a shiny, maroon Schwinn. J.P. bought one too. Then mine was stolen about two weeks later and I was depressed for weeks. I never rode a bike again until college, where I'd borrow a friend's bike to ride into town, when the weather was warm.

Every evening, after we completed our homework, we could sit in the livingroom and watch TV. The boys enjoyed shows like *The Hulk* and *The Six Million Dollar Man*. My favorite shows were *The Cosby Show, The Jeffersons, Ironside* and *All In The Family*. I adored *The Cosby Show* because it portrayed a family where everyone is loved and equally reprimanded. My favorite character was Claire Huxtable, played by Phylicia Rashad, whose voice makes motherhood a sacred gift to humanity. We were also encouraged to watch educational TV events too, like *Roots*. Ma made sure that we saw each and every episode. I was glad I did because not only did it make me sound intelligent when we discussed it in class but I also felt gratitude and reverence for my ancestors. I learned a poignant and significant piece of Black history rarely taught in school.

My favorite class was English and my least favorite was history. I simply was not feeling the connection between the "then and now." So, admittedly, I was just going through the motions memorizing dates and other facts. Thus, in all my subjects, I made the honor roll in jr. high and high school. Award ceremonies were like The Oscars® for me, especially in jr. high school where I'd clean up on academic awards in Science and English.

Saturdays, I watched *Soul Train* so that I could keep up with the latest dance steps. We also participated in community African culture sessions filled with dance, music, crafts and academics. Sometimes, when there was a Jack and Jill function I would go and experience what it meant to be a "cultured" girl. And sometimes we would check out a movie. Other times the Vaughan's relatives would visit and we would all eat, chat and play with the cousins. One of my favorite people was Grandma Jessie, who lived in Center Moriches. Each time we visited her, she would have already cooked and when we entered her immaculate, wall-to-wall carpeted home, we were enveloped by the freshest and richest aroma of soul food, which included Grandma Jessie's famous homemade coconut cake. This would always make me think of my own grandmother, but since I didn't think I'd ever hear or see Daddy's mother again, I secretly replaced her with Grandma Jessie. She was so funny she'd have us rolling on the floor. Grandma Jessie had the funniest words and phrases like "trickums" to describe the male genitals, and "packah" to describe the female organ. When she felt sorry for someone she would say, "Oh, the po' critture!". Grandma Jessie had a huge backyard with a beautiful apple tree and an outhouse.

I was invited to Grandma Jessie's funeral in May 1995 just before her ninetieth birthday that June. She died after her husband, a wonderful man named Rudolph, who passed away a few years before. I could tell from the eulogy the impact Grandma Jessie had on the lives of other people. She had lived a happy and full life.

Family members from all sides attended the packed but beautiful funeral. It was like a mini family reunion—one I had always wanted for my own family. This one for Grandma Jessie more than sufficed.

Sundays were set aside for the family to read the paper. We would all lounge around wherever we chose, and read the Sunday paper. As a teacher and private tutor years later, I required that my students read the paper even if it were only one article per day, because I knew it would expand their level of comprehension, vocabulary, writing skills and world view. All of my students excelled.

My favorite Sunday meals included smothered pork chops or ham hocks, rice, potatoes, or dumplings, lima beans and cabbage. To this day, I will not eat potato salad other than Ma's. Anyhow, we'd devour everything because Ma cooked, not me, even though she'd let me help prep the food like peel potatoes and clean and chop vegetables. Ma even taught me how to make piecrust from scratch.

Yes, there was order, stability, entertainment, culture and J.P. in my life. All the makings of a "well-rounded" foster home. What more could I ask?

◆   ◆   ◆

In 1971 my father came to see us. It was the happiest day of my life. I had not seen him for about two years. Once again, I would be queen. 'He came back, he's here, he kept his promise!' I'd thought. Daddy brought a white blanket for the Vaughan's as a gift. He exchanged pleasantries then briefly spoke to J.P. and spent most of his time with me. We reminisced and talked about my cousins and other family members. He told me that everyone was fine including Grandma. I remember feeling joy when I heard that Grandma was alive and well. Before he left, Daddy promised me that once he "got things straight" he would come back for me…soon.

Months and years went by before I realized I would not hear from my father again. I had to finally face the cold, hard bitter truth:

I had become a bonified foster child.
It seemed like I didn't belong
to my self. I felt like a ghost
that just hangs around, drifting aimlessly
until one day it finds a real body,
a body full of love, confidence
and fun to be around.

The word "foster" became an invisible shadow that followed me throughout my adolescent years. I hated when we all went out together to the supermarket or to do laundry—you know, places where you'll more than likely see your neighbors and peers. "And who are *they?*" folks would ask, noticing no resemblance, especially me, since I was darkest. I would have felt somewhat liberated if Ma and Dad said something like, 'None of your damn business!' I hated when there would be rumors in school that I was a foster child and students would say, "I heard you're a foster child, is that *true?*" or ask, "You're a *foster* child?!" Some wouldn't even know the difference between foster care and adoption and would ask, "I heard you're *adopted*. Is that *true?*"

"No", I'd reply out loud but in my head I'd add 'dumbass!' Then, I'd explain with excruciating shame masked by a nervous smile just so they would leave me alone: "I'm just living there (with the Vaughan's) *temporarily*...they're sort of like my fake family until I go back to mine" desperately hoping that this would be true.

Each time my social worker, Mr. Saunders, came for routine home visits, I hoped he would say something like: 'Your father is coming to pick you up' or 'soon you can go home to your *real* family.' Instead, he'd awkwardly ask the standard question: "Sssooo, how's everything?" and I would give a standard answer saying, "Everything's fine..." knowing full well, on a deeper level, I was suffering inside and I didn't want to be there much longer.

Agency visits tortured me. J.P. and I would be picked up in the agency car and driven for what seemed like hours to Manhattan, only to return disappointed. Not one family member showed up. The agency would keep us busy with toys, games, TV and "seeing someone." Then we would have lunch—a sandwich, milk and cookies then go home. This routine occurred time and again, and each time I would feel more 'broke', busted and disgusted than the last.

I felt *poor* even though the Vaughan's were very financially stable. I felt a deep sense of lack *inside* and this emptiness colored my attitude and view about myself, life and what it means to be responsible, especially in the area of money where I created a pattern of gain and loss, mostly loss.

◆   ◆   ◆

In order to maintain whatever sanity I could find within myself, I tried to divert attention away from my foster shadow by creating a different identity; one that would make classmates and friends think that I was ok, normal, fun to be with. I would also try to fit in with students who were smart but popular. They had to be smart because I was smart, having made the honor rolls in Algebra, English and Science in jr. high and high school. I was also a member of the Drama Club. I wanted to be an actress because I thought it would make me feel pretty and I thought it would be a great outlet for deeply embedded feelings. Ma was supportive of my performing in church skits and school plays but pointed out that successful performers "began their career as babies." So I thought I wouldn't stand a chance and I squashed the idea.

Being smart gave me an interim sense of validation and confidence since I felt that I didn't have anything else going for me. I felt ugly because I "looked like a foster child," (according to a woman social worker some years later when I worked at a family service agency. The woman described an obnoxius teen living in kinship foster care, as "looking like a foster child"). For me this meant appearing homely-looking, raggedy or needy, even though none of this was true while living with the Vaughan's. As a matter of fact, when I turned sixteen, Ma suggested that I start to explore wearing make-up so that I didn't "look like a plain Jane," she'd say. I dipped and dabbed in Valarie's make-up, when she lived with us for a while. Valarie was pretty and when she applied her makeup, not too much, not too little, she'd look like a movie star. So, one day I tried to apply eyeliner and mascara. When we all sat down for dinner,

Will gave me this strange look and asked, "What happened to your eye?" It did look like someone punched me in the face and gave me a black eye. "Nothing," I said, wishing the question was something like, "You look pretty!" To make matters worse, "Iris" had reared her ugly head again. So, for a while I couldn't wear any eye makeup which made me feel even uglier.

Once, a doctor told Ma that "Iris" was psychosomatic. I wanted to slap him. The pain I was feeling was real. Tell someone who is suffering from a migraine headache that it's psychosomatic and see how they respond! "Iris" got on my last nerve until my freshman year in college, when I discovered taking Tylenol gave me relief from headaches and eye pain due to the inflammation somewhere behind my eyeball. The eye karma I'd suffer with for about two or three years was finally over, and it didn't leave me blind or deformed. Thank God! But I still felt ugly.

It didn't help that J.P. and Will would call me names like pancake because I have a flat forehead—it doesn't bulge out, and, as was the sport amongst others in the neighborhood, they would call me every black spot, spook, dot, pan, tire, snake, etc. they could think of. I actually thought my complexion was the exact same color as a black crayon until one day, in my fifth-grade art class, we were instructed to draw our faces with colored chalk. I drew an oval-shaped head with hair that looked like Medea. Then I drew some lips and colored them with red chalk for lipstick. I drew my eyes and a poor rendition of glasses. Then I picked up a stick of the darkest chalk and proceeded to color my face in the charcoal-black color, leaving the whites of my eyes covered by glasses. The art teacher walked around examining each student's artwork and exclaiming how great they were doing. When she stopped by my desk, there was momentary silence and then she graciously asked me if I really thought I was that color. I was startled. Without waiting for my answer, she invited me to look into the floor length mirror we had in the back of the room. After studying myself for a about a minute, I immediately went back to my desk and redrew my face using the most appropriate shade of brown available.

I'm not sure if the picture was hung up with the others or if I took it home and hung it up in my room. I do know that I felt better about the reality of my complexion. Nowadays, I look and feel pretty, especially when I eat delicious, nutritious foods, excercise—I play paddleball, swim and walk *a lot!*—and take the time to adorn my body with beautiful clothes and pleasant fragrances. I have grown to love my chocolate, supple body and I am blessed to say that nothing has been

deleted, nipped, tucked
augmented, burnt out nor poked with
needles full of @#$%&!
i have all my teeth, even the wise ones
and i can stretch limb to limb
yes, i love my healthy, 5 foot, 3 inch
shapely, chocolate frame
with gracefully long feet that respect past travels
and look forward to the journeys ahead....

When I stopped complaining and reacting to J.P., Will and other people calling me names, it stopped, especially when I started high school, where fellas began to show interest in me. Ma and Dad would watch me like hawks and rightly so—they could see that I was getting ready to go buck wild. I knew that they did not want me to have any "accidents" so I avoided serious relationships until late in my senior year.

Carolyn and Marlene were straight A students. I especially liked Marlene. Carolyn was a little too classy for my taste. Marlene was a few years younger than me but she was cool, mature. Marlene and Carolyn lived with their parents, a German woman and an African-American man who lived one block over, behind us, on the other side of our fence. You could clearly see the family barbecue food and swim in their enticing pool in the summertime.

Marlene and I talked a lot about life and spirituality and we'd drink beer together. One New Year's eve I was home alone, so I called Marlene then slipped over to her house. Ma and Dad had gone to a dance. Whenever they went out, they'd get decked out enough to be in a fashion show with the likes of Naomi Campbell and Tyra Banks. Will had gone out with friends, and J.P. had visited a friend or neighbor. I was at Marlene's for about an hour getting juiced until twelve midnight, when we saw the ball drop on TV. Then I went home and crashed.

When I turned sixteen, Marlene and Carolyn came to my sweet sixteen party held in our unfurnished but neat and clean basement. I was jealous of Carolyn because I knew she would get all the guys and requests for a dance. Some neighbors and school friends came too. We danced, played games and ate the usual—cake, ice cream and munchies. Then, as was the custom at parties, someone unscrewed the regular light bulb and put in a red one. Next thing you know folks were either grinding to slow music or in a corner smooching—except Marlene and me. So I didn't feel so bad. I still enjoyed myself and felt a new sense of maturity, especially since I knew I'd be on my own in two years.

Vickie was voted prom queen. She had beauty, brains and was very popular in high school. Vickie loved people. We became friends when we worked together one summer at a neighborhood community center. Vickie was one of the few people Ma and Dad allowed me to hang with. So I hung out with her hoping to discover her winning formula. I was surprised Vickie let me hang with her sometimes and she never disrespected me. The best thing I liked about Vickie was she never viewed me as a foster child. She simply saw me as a friend or a hangin' buddy.

Vickie even had the perfect man, Anthony. He was tall and fine like Michael Jordan, and he had a car. Sometimes we'd cool out at Vickie's house or Anthony would drive us to a movie. We'd always have a "bag" and some papers.

Vickie knew how to party and have fun. Sometimes Vickie, I and some friends would go dancing then off to White Castle or IHop afterwards. Once, Valarie drove us, at my request, to a nice club on Long Island and hung out with us. We all had a nice time. I had always wanted to hang out with Val, as if she were my big sister.

Soon it was time to graduate from Amityville Memorial High. I bought a yearbook and I made sure I collected as many signatures as possible from friends and others I did not know so well. The signatures were proof that I could win everyone's favor despite my foster-handicap. I believe being friends with Vickie helped. I was even invited to a graduation party.

Vickie was going to Brandeis and I was going to work during the summer before I'd be leaving Amityville for a new and far, far away scene. 'Soon I am going to be independent! I will meet new friends and date a basketball player,' I'd thought.

Sociology 101

The sun's healing rays
gently massages my wounded ego.
As the sun-laced sky
fades into an impeccable
royal blue,
my mind instructs its masquerades
to fade to black.
—From *Sacred Blues, Poetry*

1978. Lake Ontario was located behind the Scales, Briggs, Johnson and Waterbury dorms at SUNY Oswego. Oswego State is one of the largest and most beautiful campuses in the SUNY system. The spring and summer seasons in Oswego are cooler than New York City weather but crisp and very clear enough to see the border of Canada if you ventured behind the Scales, Briggs, Johnson and Waterbury dorms. Breathtaking sunsets and the song of the waves from the lake were my refuge away from the challenge of college life.

We really didn't have a Fall season, and winters were challenging to those of us who had never experienced such consistently extremely cold temperatures and very deep snow. It snowed at least three feet and temperatures fell below zero. If you washed your hair and went outside without a hat your hair would become frozen locs. In seconds your hands were numb. We were lucky to have a shuttle

bus that stopped not far from our dorm, about every twenty minutes, to facilitate travel to class.

◆   ◆   ◆

There were very few African-American students during my first
semester. Most of us were from the New York City area, mainly the
Bronx, Manhattan and Brooklyn.

Nadine, Ivelisse and Fran lived down the hall and around the corner from me in Oneida Hall, a co-ed dorm. All of us were the only
women of color in our wing if not in the entire dorm at that time.
Nadine, Ivelisse and Fran had come for the summer session to get a
head start, so they knew the deal: who was who, stores in the area,
etc. I met Cheryl, our other friend, later. She lived in Mooreland,
way north on the other side of campus.

Nadine, Ivelisse and Fran welcomed me with open arms, and
always had my back especially when I had experienced racist pranks,
like the time I went to the bathroom and saw a black doll hanging
from a shower stall. Another time, there was a racial slur imprinted
on a banner made from computer paper that was taped along one of
the walls near my room. Ivelisse and Fran saw the banner and peeled
it down. They were cool, no violence, but pressed me to complain
to the floor RA (resident advisor). We went as a united front and the
blatant incidents stopped, even though there were still those who
felt they had the right to intimidate, like the stare-downs in the
bathroom when I brushed my teeth. Instead of a smile or a hello
when our eyes met, I'd just get stared at until I stared back sardoni-
cally. I had graduated from a high school full of students from every
walk of life, so I thought going to Oswego State would be a piece of
cake.

I had not experienced the quickly expanding diversity of Oswego State until my sophomore year. There were student organizations or student unions for every nationality on campus—the Latin Student Union, Jewish Student Union, International Student Union, and the Black Student Union—which threw some of the best parties, complete with delicious food and music that brought *everyone* together. Still, for many of us African-American students, Oswego State was "Oz"—keg parties, barfing (vomiting), and all. It was another world many of us had never experienced.

When I needed a break from the game of campus life, I ventured down the rocks behind the Scales, Briggs, Johnson and Waterbury dorms. I would also maintain my sanity by going to the campus library after classes. We could select an album and listen on a headset that was provided. I always listened to Earth, Wind, and Fire. My favorite cut was *The Way of the World*. I would sit for hours listening to the entire album, at least twice. Afterwards, feeling a little blissed out but more focused, I would return to my dorm room and stay there studying until dinnertime, or until Nadine, Cheryl, Ivelisse and Fran came and plucked me out of my room.

It did not take long for me to get the hang of the college routine but I was not as prepared as I thought to face a more mature population of students, particularly the handful of African-American students who were members of the Black Student Union. The BSU produced events that included prominent speakers, and hosted parties where all students were invited. There would be private room parties too, where I learned how to play backgammon and smoke weed through my nose.

I was growing impatient, though. Instead of allowing myself to grow, and slowly gel with the others, I felt threatened. The other women seemed more mature-looking than me. And, they had already claimed their man, or bed partner. Well, I wanted a man too. But I was a "bull in a china shop." And too arrogant to even notice. People were trying to befriend me, and I was turning possibilities into war. I was only concerned about myself. I wanted to be desired and feel like a woman. After all, I would be away from home for four years, so I had lots of freedom to explore. I went a little too far in my exploration, though.

Nadine, Cheryl, Ivelisse and Fran were my friends, the only ones who stuck with me, the only ones who accepted me for me, even though I was moody and had an attitude. They nicknamed me Button because I was so unpredictable. Anyhow, they scolded me about being an easy lay. They said I should have more class about dating. The disgust on their faces made me think twice.

One day all of us had gone to the campus cafeteria to have lunch. The topics ranged from professors' quirks, test scores, getting a ride home, the next stipend, parties and who was doing the nasty with whom. After a while, everyone left except me and a Brother about the size of Mr. T. We talked for a while when suddenly, out of the blue, he said, "I'd like to go to bed with you." I was stunned at first, then flattered that he at least asked me nicely but I was shocked at the thought of being squashed like Ms. Purdy was by Professor Clump in Eddie Murphy's *The Nutty Professor*, during the beach scene. I gasped, "No" and scurried off with my tray. I told my friends, who looked at me with an egg on their face expression and fell out laughing.

I didn't date anyone until the spring, when I met Edwin. He arrived during my second or third semester. Ed was tall and had a beautiful deep complexion. He was funny and so smart that he could get high the night before a test and still pull an A. I was surprised and moved especially because of the sweet manner in which he asked me to be his girlfriend, on a beautiful early fall afternoon. I was proud of myself. I had become a woman.

Ed was popular. Tony was his roommate and both got along very well. Ed and Tony were from New York City, like others who became friends with them—Janys, Yasmin, Marcia, Steve C., Sally, Elsie, Lisa, Chris and others. I got to know Janys and some of her friends a little better by typing their papers for a Black history class. In addition to making some extra cash, I seized the opportunity to prove myself as a friend by typing papers. (Ma knew what she was doing when she suggested I take a typing class in high school). Every crew has its beloved leader and Janys was it. So I figured if I won Janys's friendship, I was "in".

Janys was a lot of fun. She was like another Vickie, my high school friend, only much taller. But my attention soon shifted towards Lisa. Lisa was like Vickie too but a little moody like me, yet her moods didn't have the nasty edge mine did and she didn't lose friends. Lisa behaved like a classy lady. So I thought I could learn something from her.

It would take a while, though, before I would understand the effect my attitude had on others. But I wanted to be so right about *expecting* people to understand and accept me just as I was, I could have lifted a thousand pounds with one pinky! This attitude effected my relationship with almost every roommate I had. Things would start out okay but after a few weeks somehow I ended up having a nasty argument and they'd be the ones to leave. So, I was often living as a single occupant in a room designed for two to six students. I did enjoy the solitude and privacy but this didn't increase visitations at all. For many years after college I continued to develop this pattern of not getting along with people I lived with and I was always the tenant, not the one whose name was on the lease. So I would get evicted either because of my attitude or because I had developed the habit of being in debt and was often late with my portion of the rent.

I began to wake up a little when my relationship with Ed started to slowly deteriorate. One day I accused him of seeing another female or I did something he didn't like. I tried to fix it but messed up even more. He asked me to leave his room but I continued to argue to the point where he had to physically remove me from his space. I hated him for handling me that way, but I really hated myself. I was dethroned, once again.

I saw Ed a couple of years ago on a cool winter day in Harlem. We exchanged greetings and spoke briefly. He was getting married. I congratulated him and we went our separate ways. I was happy to have brought a pleasant closure to our past relationship.

After I broke up with Ed I really wasn't interested in anyone else, except Steve C. Confession: I *always* had a crush on him but he already knew how I was, so I thought I didn't even stand a chance. And I dared not ask. I was attracted to Steve's handsome features and deep complexion and especially his mature insight about life and politics.

Years after college, in the nineties, I had to obtain a passport in order to fulfill an ID requirement for a non-driver's license. I called the passport office in Manhattan and a man answered. I stated my reason for the call and he asked for my name.

"Quelyn?!"

"Y-yes?"

"This is Steve…from Oswego, remember?" Aw damn!

"Yes, how're you doing?"

"I'm alright….so where're you going?"

"Uh, well, I'm planning to go to Africa." I figured I had to lie in order to avoid further questioning about my original intent to get a passport. My mind performed all kinds of gymnastics: Should I apologize for being nasty towards him in college, and say how I really felt about him? Nah, too late. But then again, he did seem happy to hear from me. Nah, he's probably going steady with someone or married by now, besides, why would he be interested in *me*, *now* anyway? We talked for a few more minutes then we hung up. I was happy that I finally had a friendly conversation with Steve.

I chose to stick with Nadine, Cheryl, Ivelisse and Fran. All the seniors we knew had graduated. We ventured off-campus to party and meet some cool, mature people once again. I also bought a new stereo system so that I could have my own room parties and prove that I could be popular too. Some folks would come because there was totally nothing else happening or because their friends chose to come. My parties were ok. The most memorable one was the one when I had typed up funny messages on slips of paper and put each message in a balloon. Cheryl had helped me blow up balloons, by mouth. If you stood outside my room with the door closed, you would have thought we were having sex. I had said something like, "Cheryl, you're not blowing hard enough…it's got to be bigger…I think you should stick it in *before* you blow…" Anyhow, towards the end of the party, I had my guests grab a balloon from the ceiling, pop it and read their message. They got a kick out of that.

In the midst of studies and partying, I discovered that Oswego State had an excellent drama department. I enrolled in some courses and did well. The drama department produced a play called Medea, which received rave reviews. I especially remember Professor McCullough, a drama teacher who looked like Frederick Douglass. Professor McCullough directed a play about Harriet Tubman and I was invited to audition. When I was chosen to play a principle part, Harriet's mother, I felt I had come home, home to *me*. I played Harriet Tubman's mother to rave reviews. I gained respect from others and I felt more respectful within myself. Indeed, I felt like a star. I thought for sure the queen was back.

◆   ◆   ◆

The Vaughan's could not come to my graduation. I was disappointed but then I thought perhaps this was the official mama bird pushing her young out of its cozy net—and *no flying back*.

I graduated with a BA in Communication Studies and minor in Theatre. So I figured, 'Finding a job, a wonderful place to stay, and great new friends, should be pretty easy; after all, college had taught me *all* the lessons of social life and my foster care issues were finally behind me. So, no *residual pain*, no more drama.' Right?

The Real World

Oswego was not the town to seek gainful employment at the time. Jobs were scarce in the small town and since I did not drive I would need to depend on public transportation that was just as scarce as jobs were. So I called Lydia, a friend I met in college during my freshman year. We had kept in touch on and off.

I had been staying with Lydia for a short while, maybe less than a year when I found temporary work in the EOP (Economic Opportunity Program) office at Syracuse University. So I was ok for some months until they did not need me anymore. I was taking too long to find work even though Lydia could see that I was actively looking, going on interviews and all but to no avail. I even tried welfare, but the system was not having it, especially since I was fresh out of college and single with no children—I was too scared to omit the college thing and I didn't know how to lie. So, I think the most I got was some food stamps. Then those ran out. Lydia and I had an argument and I got an attitude. I felt she should have understood and been more patient. After all, it wasn't like I didn't try. But I had an attitude. So I had to leave, within days.

One evening I ventured into town and came across a club. I ordered a drink, something cheap like Rum and Coke. An attractive young woman named Sonia sat on the stool next to me. She was well groomed and I could tell by the way she was dressed that she worked at a bank or some other corporate environment. As we talked, it turned out she was a bank teller and had a family, a little boy and husband. Sonia barely took a few sips of her drink and already she was revealing details of her past which included how her man was no longer treating her right. She was vulnerable and I thought, 'Now's my chance.' Even today, people I've never seen before—adults, children and teens—reveal their stuff to me, uninvited. But it took years of practice through teaching, casework and counseling to develope the ability to be a confidante.

I returned to Lydia's that night and the next day I packed my belongings—a small boom box I had bought (I had already sold my stereo for money I needed in order to move to Syracuse), some clothes and whatever food I had left. I don't remember if Lydia was home or not but I left and went to Sonia's house.

When you move into someone else's home, especially if you are desperate, you have to live by their rules. I was stubborn. Especially when it came to my music—it was all I had to calm my nerves. So whenever I was not out job hunting I would hang out in the extra room Sonia had, and play my radio. I would only come out to make something simple to eat or to use the bathroom.

It all came to a head when I let them use my cherished box for a small cookout one day. Their guests were a little too rough with it and I bitched and complained to no avail. So when Sonia returned my boom box that night, I played my music and when they told me to turn it down I got an attitude. They let me know it too. And I had to leave.

I called Lydia. I couldn't stand the thought of being homeless. So, I apologized to Lydia stating that I realized what pulled us apart (my attitude) and that I would really make an extra effort to find work. I knew how to negotiate when my back was against the wall. Stacey, Lydia's friend, who lived down the hall, suggested that I go to the Syracuse University employment office and apply for a job. I got in as a temp in SU's financial aid office.

Working at SU gave me access to other areas and students on campus. Shortly after, having been impressed with the African-American fraternities and sororities, I pledged one of the top two sororities in the country. But since I had already graduated I had to pledge to the graduate chapter. The women were medical professionals, teachers, lawyers, dedicated and witty family women and wives. They treated me like family—something I had missed. Being in the sorority gave me a feeling of self-worth and importance. It gave me validation. Once you get plugged into a prominent membership, anything you need in life is at your fingertips. When I returned to New York, however, I became inactive. I could not afford the dues and I was still getting my life together.

One of my sorors, Pat, offered a room in her beautifully furnished basement apartment complete with a bar, which was off limits. The bar was Pat's domain.

Pat was a schoolteacher. She had a beautiful, bright little boy about eight years old, and we got along very well. Pat's home was huge and had a beautiful backyard where she tended her gardens. Life seemed to be going smoothly now for me, especially when I had another opportunity to express myself creatively. The theatre.

Winter was settling in. But this did not stop me from partying and meeting new people, especially since I worked on campus amidst the hustle and bustle of classes and entertainment of campus life at SU. I met an aspiring actor named Joe who invited me to a production meeting at the Paul Robeson Theatre Company (PRTC) in Syracuse, where he was a member. They were working on what turned out to be a hallmark production, *The Motown*

Review. I regret not remembering all who were involved but I do remember key people like Bill, the founder and director; Ron, artistic director; Annette, costume designer/actress; and Sandra, a publicist who relentlessly drove me home almost every night after rehearsals. I was a production assistant and helped with props, makeup and costumes. The PRTC gained a new level of respect and honor from the theatrical community and citizens of Syracuse, who previously thought such a magnanimous event could not be done. I was proud to be a part of its success.

Summer was drawing near and my temp job at SU was ending, so I "would no longer be needed." (I got used to hearing that phrase later in life). Once again, I had to pound the pavement. In the meantime I applied for welfare, again. I got food stamps but nothing for rent. My relationship with Pat had become intense, especially when she was drunk. But I was arrogant too, and according to Pat, ungrateful. One of our sorors intervened.

Corene was my favorite soror. She was a beautiful woman who knew how to get anyone to do what was necessary and with integrity. I admired Corene's relationship with her beautiful and smart teenage daughter and I admired the way she could be serious but light. One day Corene popped over unannounced. Pat must've called her. 'Good. I'll get to tell my side of the story,' I thought. We talked for about an hour about my childhood, college and my reluctance to contact the Vaughan's because I had already decided that their not coming to my graduation meant they were officially letting me go. They had done their job and I was on my own, never to return. The truth was that I didn't get a chance to say goodbye to the people who took care of me for eight years. So I had become resentful and had stuffed it in the attic of my mind.

Corene suggested, matter of factly, "Why don't you call them? They would probably welcome you with open arms." I'll never forget this special meeting with Corene.

Unexpected Embrace

One or two years passed before I would contact the Vaughan's. I wanted to be able to say that I was doing well in case they'd ask.

I called Tricia, a friend who lived in Queens. She invited me to live with her and her father, until I could get a job and my own place. Tricia taught me how to file a tax return and receive food stamps in the City. She and her father were gracious enough to let me be there without the pressure of having to give them money for rent.

I found work much quickly than I did in Syracuse. My first job was at an advertising agency as a secretary to account executives. Once again, I reclaimed my independence and yes, validation. But I started to squander my money on clothes, short plane trips to Syracuse to visit old friends, and other trivial things. I was so busy trying to "live large", I didn't take care to spend wisely and save generously. I'd regret not saving my money and it would be a while before I learned my lesson.

I stayed with Tricia for about a year or less because, you guessed it, I had a fight. I don't remember if it was jealousy or something I said or did or didn't do. My guess in hindsight is that I got arrogant, again, and it appeared as though I was not grateful to Tricia and her father for taking me in.

At this point, since I was so close to home, Amityville, I had to call Ma and Dad. I felt terrible. I did not want this first call since graduation to be one of desperation. I quickly found a place in Far

Rockaway *then* I called Ma and Dad. Corene was right. They were, indeed, very happy to hear from me. After I had told them about how nice graduation was and how glad I was to have completed school and received my degree, I explained that I was not getting along with my new roommate and that her family requested that I leave. The best part about my situation was that Ma and Dad neither criticized the situation nor did they make Tricia or me wrong. Instead, they offered that I could come home and have my room back as long as I was willing to buy my own food. This sounded like a good deal. Now, if only I had a car and knew how to drive. I sincerely appreciated my parent's gesture but I knew this arrangement would not be practical for me because I would have to use the Long Island Railroad to commute to my job in Manhattan. I wasn't financially ready to incur this kind of expense. I did come home for the night and the next day Ma and Dad drove me to my new spot in Far Rockaway.

As it turned out, though, the townhouse I moved into was roach-infested, had limited cooking facilities and the bathroom was constantly filthy. Furthermore, I did not like the idea of riding the train on what seemed like a long stretch of tracks in the middle of a wide body of water, which was the Jamaica Bay. This scared the hell out of me for a while until I saw the indifference on the faces of the other passengers. Then I figured, 'What the hell, I *can* swim if anything should happen, so get over it.' Yeah, right!

Reunited, Didn't Feel So Good

While I was desperately searching for a new apartment, I also longed to get back into the theatre scene. I had become hungry again, wanting to revisit the "high" I got from being with the Paul Robeson Performing Arts Company. So, I called Directory Assistance to inquire about other African-American theatres in the New York City area. The male voice kindly gave me the number to the National Black Theatre (NBT) in Harlem. I called NBT and Tunde, the Director of Theatre Arts and an award-winning producer, answered the phone. I explained who I was and the story of how I got NBT's number. Without hesitation, Tunde graciously invited me to "be a part of the NBT family."

I visited NBT when it was in the middle of rehearsals for the original Audelco Award-winning *Nzinga's Children*. They needed someone to create whip marks on Old Nzinga's back. I volunteered and I was given the chance to do makeup with encouragement and coaching from the cast and crew. The whip marks proved to be very effective.

Tunde passed away in August 2001. He left us with a powerful declaration that he used to say to many of us who found wisdom in his love and commitment to humanity and Black people: "I'm in the game, still playing."

◆   ◆   ◆

I moved into the furnished basement of a woman's home not far from where Tricia lived, in Springfield Gardens. I had convinced the woman that I was working and could pay rent on time and in full.

I was still working at the advertising agency in 1985 when I called the Army and was finally in touch with my brother, Private Purdie. I remained in touch whenever I could until later when he was discharged. J.P. called me one day and said that he needed a place to stay until he got himself together. 'Hell yeah!' I'd thought. I would finally be reunited with a major link in my life. I was hoping, this time, we'd never be torn apart again. Plus, I loved the idea of having protection. I had no doubt that if I needed J.P. to confront any man who disrespected me, J.P. could take care of business.

I arrived at Port Authority at the place J.P. said to expect him. My brother was very strong and healthy and he looks like LL Cool J, dimples and all. Anyhow, we spotted one another almost at the same time. J.P. plopped his huge duffle bag down, lifted me up, squeezed me and swung me around. I was ecstatic. I had not seen my brother for about ten or fifteen years. But we were back. I silently vowed to never let him slip through my fingers again.

I didn't realize how much I cherished solitude, privacy and cleanliness until I discovered how attached J.P. was to the habits of Army life, like being funky for awhile and sleeping crunched up in a small space—like the loveseat in my apartment. "I'm used to being in fox holes…" J.P. would announce, when I pleaded for him to sleep in my bed which was big enough for the both of us.

I had not given him a chance. For him, I had become a "nag". J.P. always disliked nagging, even when we lived with the Vaughan's. Ma would reprimand us about something several times (because some of us were hard-headed) and J.P. saw this as nagging. J.P. had been living with me for less than a month when one day I started a very bad argument, unintentionally, and I ended up kicking him out. When I calmed down, I felt like crap.

J.P. was gone for a couple of days, and slept wherever he could. I regretted not being more understanding of who my brother had become. I was angry at myself and I felt guilty. How could I treat him this way after all the things we've gone through as children, especially my father's reluctance to accept him as his own son! My heart ached worse than when the agency first came for J.P. when we were little, because this time, my losing him *again* would be *my* fault.

One evening J.P. rang my doorbell. I knew it was he. The bell sounded contrite. I opened the door and he asked if he could come back. I gladly conceded but I requested that we talk things out in order for us to live in harmony. And so it was.

The advertising company had budget problems and I was laid off. Shortly after, they closed shop. I explained to my landlord that I was looking for work, but she wouldn't hear of it. Once again, I was in crisis. I was desperate.

Janys and I had kept in contact with one another over the years, especially when I moved to Queens. But this time it would be a call for help. Janys offered me a place with her aunt on Amsterdam Avenue in Harlem, as long as I would monitor her and help out when needed. I always wanted to live in Manhattan, one of the greatest towns in the world.

J.P. and I were getting along fine and I invited him to live with me. He explained that he had met a young lady while he was out looking for work and that he planned to either live with her or return to the Service. I was disappointed, but I knew that if he wanted and needed to contact me he could because I told him where I'd be.

I'm still looking for him.

Detox

Late spring or early summer of 1986, I read about a biochemist who owned an institute for natural health in Brooklyn. He was known for healing people through herbal extracts and a vegetarian diet. I decided to check it out. I had not been back to Brooklyn since I was a little girl living with Daddy and Grandma.

The biochemist's assistants looked beautiful. They wore no makeup to cover their healthy complexions and they displayed a confident, pleasant and peaceful demeanor. I wanted that too. So, under the biochemist's guidance I became a vegetarian. No sugar, dairy, and nothing that swims, walks, flies or oinks. I gave it up effortlessly, especially the meat and fish. I gave up dairy "cold turkey" but found that it would take a little more discipline to renounce it all—I was still attached to pizza and Haagen Dazs.

I met my best friend, Robert, at the institute. I immensely value Robert's friendship because, although we don't agree on everything, he respects my opinions and he has always respected me as a woman. Robert is there for me through thick and thin. When others I consider friends will not respond or are not available, Robert is there for me. Robert is a great father too. He reared two beautiful, grown children who are healthy and prosperous people of fine character.

I discovered that being a vegetarian combined with exercise not only strengthened my body but significantly increased my energy level, awareness and improved my physical appearance. I am healthier now than I was at 16. I also learned how to heal or "cleanse" myself whenever my body experiences discomfort like a headache, a cough, sniffles, or an ache or pain. I am not always thrilled with the repercussions of my "older than I look" appearance, though. Sometimes people approach me or start speaking to me as though I am a clueless teenager until I say something intelligent or reveal my age. Then they stare at me as though I have three heads.

Grace Bestowed

In summer 1986, I was invited to attend a meditation program held at the Manhattan Center in downtown Manhattan.

I arrived just in time to hear the last thirty or so minutes of the talk by Gurumayi Chidvilasananda, a world-renowned meditation master. She told a beautiful story about how we tend to impose our love onto others and *expect* them to accept it.

When the truth hits, either you surrender to it or you fight—and continue to look like a fool. I sat there, in the packed hall and

sobbed like a child
who watched her sand castle
dissolve
under the weight of a
truth unknown.
I flew out of my own hell so fast
I didn't have time to
think, analyze, conceptualize
nor theorize how I was released.
I was released from myself
to my Self.

After the talk, I was invited to meet Gurumayi whose beautiful big brown eyes welcomed me with the most *knowing* and benevolent glance. No words were exchanged but I knew that we would meet again.

A few years later, I enrolled in my first meditation intensive with Gurumayi in South Fallsburg, New York. An intensive is a course containing the desired information which is usually crammed into a two-day period or a shorter-than-normal period of time. I learned *how* to meditate by focusing on my breath, and sitting in a comfortable erect posture. Then we were instructed on *what* to meditate: God, the Self, consciousness, or whatever you prefer to call the inexplicable velvety sense of unconditional love and silence I experienced inside.

Through the prescribed meditation practices, I gained the courage to boldly confront the tendency to remain stuck in old patterns of thinking and being that previously left me feeling sorry for myself. And remember *all* the social skills I claimed to have learned in college? It was all just "the tip of the iceberg"! I grew to accept the possibility of learning something new *every* day.

In addition to the practice of meditation one is encouraged to do seva (selfless service) which is basically performed in honor of the life-transforming spiritual teachings a mediation master reveals to devotees. I extended the practice of seva to my community especially during the holidays. I developed the habit of bringing food to a homeless person on Thanksgiving Day or Christmas. I can't describe the immense satisfaction I got from making a contribution like this to another human being in need—someone who could very well have been me. There's something very powerful about feeding others.

Very soon, holidays were no longer a source of lonliness or a reminder of the pain I'd suffer as a child longing to spend the time with her own biological family. As a matter of fact, I was now being invited to eat and be with friends and other families. Sometimes students I have tutored would invite me to be with their family.

The icing on the cake, though, was that I eventually re-established relations with Ma and Dad Vaughan. I surprised them in 2001, when I accompanied Valarie on a roadtrip to North Carolina to see them for Thanksgiving. They greeted me with open arms and we all had a great time. We still keep in touch.

Still, one of the most important lessons that I discovered is that the separation from my biological family and the events that followed, were blessings on the yellow-brick-road toward a life of learning and joy. Self-reconciliation, understanding and forgiveness rekindled my ability to feel connected—connected to all who took care of me and anyone else I'd meet…even troubled youth.

Spofford

Janys's aunt's health had become worse and the family placed her in a home. At the request of the family, the super allowed me to stay in the apartment for about a year, during which time I started work at the former Spofford Juvenile Detention Center in the Bronx. It's now called The Bridges Juvenile Center.

Spofford was just one-half hour away on the Bx6 bus that stopped around the corner on 155th Street and Amsterdam Avenue. The commute was easy, but my students were another trip. A trip that challenged my stereotypes and perception about teenagers. My students challenged every part of my being, even my newfound spirituality. I had previously worked in head start programs, elementary schools and had become an entrepreneur doing some consulting work with other youth organizations. None of this prepared me for Spofford. I had two lifelines, though, who were always available to coach and support me when I needed it. Connie, a teacher whose class was next to mine; and Grace, who was in charge of security and gave me insight about the nature of the student population at Spofford.

The students were required to attend class in the academy while they were detained until trial and transferal to another facility, usually a maximum-security prison. The students at Spofford were people who had been on the streets for most of their lives. They were thieves, drug dealers, larcenists, and they were people who bragged about how many "bodies they got." For them, Spofford was jail. For me, they were my students.

Our job was to provide a creative academic curriculum according to the grade level and age group we were dealing with. My class consisted mostly of males aged fourteen through eighteen, most of whom read, if at all, on a first grade level. I designed my class with a science section, math, reading, cultural history and recreation. Later, we were required to include AIDS awareness in our curriculum.

Each classroom was also equipped with two huge yellow footpads built into the floor for teachers to step, no, *stomp* on in case of an emergency, like a fight or assault on a teacher. The door would pop open and security would bust into the room and intervene. I had to stomp on my footpads a few times when students about twice my size would start fighting, mostly out of frustration towards a lawyer who did not show up for their trial or because of some rivalry in their dorm. One day, I had to handle something more grotesque and insulting than a fight.

I was a substitute teacher for another class of students who were a little older than the students in my class. There were only about five or six, so I thought it would be simple to manage. The average class size was about fifteen. The students were to do the reading assignment left by the absent teacher. Some complied and the others wanted to do something else, like draw or play a game. No problem. But there was one student who got down on the floor and lay on his back. I thought, 'Quelyn, just leave him alone, at least he's quiet.' I continued the lesson with the other students. About five minutes later, the student on the floor rose and approached me with a small piece of paper and a sardonic grin on his face. "Here, Miss Purdie, this is for you." A glob of semen. The Lord expresses Himself through us, in many ways. His "homegirl" aspect sprung out of me in all her glory and cursed that six-foot two hundred pound boy out, *then* she stomped on the yellow footpads. If I had gotten fired, I would have totally understood. But I didn't.

Spofford was a major turning point in my career as a teacher. I realized my students were people who never had a chance at childhood and instead, found role models in the streets. The scary part was they were the could've-been-Quelyns if she had not been rescued by the nosy neighbor in her building.

I viewed my class as human beings who needed and craved love, play, and learning—things they'd missed as children. My students enjoyed conversations about life, death, and spirituality—things I was learning on my own spiritual journey.

Six months was enough, though. I could not hang after about six months of trying to balance my newfound spiritual pursuit with the intense, oftentimes volatile student environment at Spofford. When I left, Connie, the teacher in the class next to mine, later told me that my class "flipped"—they demolished the classroom.

My experience at Spofford, and later as a caseworker for teens in kinship foster care, dispelled any fear and misconceptions about teenagers. I enjoy their company, wisdom, freedom and creativity, and I respect their concerns and issues. More importantly, I learned to win their trust by keeping my word.

Walking Through The Fire On Fire To a Tall, Cool Drink

My time was up at Janys's aunt's apartment so I had to move. But what else was new? I had become an expert by now. I moved around between Manhattan and the Bronx, living with people I had befriended. I must've moved about eight times that year, 1991.

I worked temp jobs and did some freelance work as a tutor and childcare provider but this would not bring in consistent income. So, I was scorned and kicked out—and rightly so. I had to really contemplate my situation and life at that point. I asked myself some questions until I was able to answer one of them with complete resolve and honesty. Should I just accept this way of living as my karma? Does being spiritual and loving God mean living in a constant state of struggle? Am I living my life with *integrity* right now? This was the "ah-ha!"

I discovered that I was truly physically tired of bouncing all over creation and I resolved to break this pattern of crisis and instability in my life, and clean up the trail of scornful relationships I'd left behind.

I got a job doing casework for teens at a foster care/preventive service agency in the Bronx. I had also moved back to Manhattan into a beautiful apartment with a woman who turned out to be my favorite roommate and one of the most influential people in my life. Lizan. She was, and still is, a great listener especially when I'd share poignant stories about my casework job. She'd offer insight. I'd listen.

I figured I had severed my pattern of instability, having worked at the agency for three years and lived with Lizan for just as long, when the agency experienced major financial improprieties that lead to delayed pay for about two months.

I left the agency and collected unemployment. As my benefit period came to a close, I started temp work again which had become more sporadic as the market called for advanced computer skills that I did not have. My portion of the rent was not a lot but I was finding it increasingly difficult to keep my word. This time, I did not want Lizan to have to kick me out. I couldn't end such a valuable roommate relationship on another scornful note as I had done in other situations. I moved out to a room in another building around the corner on Edgecombe.

I moved again, though, after about two weeks. The man I was renting from had not kept his word about renovating the kitchen and bathroom. He'd also sexually harassed a female tenant. Meanwhile, I could not have a phone installed because it would cost too much to install an entirely new phone line. I had to use a pay phone down the street about seven minutes away, in order to call for temp work. Each time I called, either there was no work or I'd learn that I could not be reached and my assignment had gone to someone else.

One day, after I called in for work to no avail, I returned to my room, cried for about ten minutes then chanted my prayer. Once again, I was eligible for unemployment, but this time I made a vow: to never live in crisis again.

I had kept in contact with Linda, a colleague at a preventive service agency in the Bronx. She had just gotten married and bought a brownstone on 149th Street and Amsterdam, not far from my Edgecombe spot. I explained my dilemma to Linda and she revealed that she and her husband were looking to rent two kitchenettes in their home.

I lived on 149th Street almost five years, the longest I've ever lived anywhere, barring Jefferson Avenue.

I had been collecting unemployment benefits when an acquaintance told me about a possible job in the box office of the world-renowned Riverside Church. I worked for about two months when the assignment ended. So did my benefits. When I did not receive a check I panicked, and called the unemployment office as I sat on my bed. I requested an extension to no avail. They could only suggest welfare as an alternative. I hung up the phone and as I took a deep breath something very beautiful happened. I felt embraced by a deep sense of peace, a silence where, for about two minutes, there were no thoughts, only my breath flowing evenly in and out of my body.

I was not new to this experience because of the spiritual practices I was already doing, but the beauty of it was the *effortlessness of the experience*, the *spontaneity*. It just happened without my even thinking about it.

Literally, moments later I got a call from The Riverside Church Theatre General Manager. She needed someone to sell tickets and manage the box office for another event.

This is the "tall, cool drink" I experience quite often in my life now, especially when I remember my own power within, when I remember Grace.

Meeting Angela

I have since worked my way up to full-time permanent work as an administrative assistant in the Mission & Social Justice Office where we co-sponsor events involving high-profile politicians, spiritual leaders, and activists. My favorite event happened in March 2001. The topic was, Women In Prison, a multimedia lecture and presentation by the one and only Angela Davis. The program was held in the Nave, the beautiful main sanctuary of The Riverside Church. I thought, '*Finally*, I will get to meet one of the most revered women of the sixties'—since I never got the chance to march or raise my little fist and holler the words "Black power!"

Part of my job was to research and get updated information about Angela Davis, so that if I needed to, I could speak intelligently about who she is and what she stands for today. I had seen pictures of Angela Davis and got an occasional glimpse of her on TV, but she appeared even more beautiful and humble in person, yet powerful, still.

The Women In Prison event was very successful. There was standing room only. I was most intrigued by Angela Davis's ability to attract a diverse audience of mostly young adults from every walk of life and "flava", who were freely *being* and communicating with one another…with no stigma attached.

Damita Jo, Harlem, New York!

Remember when I said that I would tell you about how I stood face to face with Janet Jackson—almost two decades after seeing her in concert with her brothers, when I was a little girl?

I was shopping for CD's at the HMV Music Store in Harlem and as I was leaving the store, I saw a poster advertising Janet's appearance. It stated that on the following Tuesday, March 30th the first seven hundred and fifty people who bought a Damita Jo CD would receive a Damita Jo backpack and a wristband. The wristband was the real ticket to meeting Janet the next day, March 31st at 4pm.

I'm not the type of person who stands on line for hours to meet anyone. So I arrived about 12:30pm. The line began at the entrance of the HMV Music Store and extended south, towards 116th Street. My spot was in the middle of 125th and 124th Streets, closer to 125th. Perhaps I had great timing or it was the dreary afternoon that impeded many more people from showing up. The temperature was about 40 and windy with light rain.

I befriended some people who stood on line behind me and despite the weather, we networked, shared Janet stories, shared a few laughs, and when any of us needed to take a walk or grab a bite to eat we'd watch the other's spot.

People came from all over. One woman and a friend had just arrived from California and would be leaving that evening. Another woman drove from Connecticut and would also return home that evening.

Around 5pm, the line began to move, quickly. The excitement grew but was contained by tight security and organization. Within minutes my new friends and I approached the entrance to the store where security guards checked for the coveted wristband on each person. If you did not have one you were told to leave, no exceptions.

Minutes became seconds as we were guided into the store, onto the escalator, and once we were at the top we were instructed by more security to have, in full view, items we wanted Janet to sign. Almost everyone had a camera and my friends and I had already discussed how we'd snap shots of one another with Janet once we got our turn to meet her.

We could see Janet, gracefully chatting with people and signing items in the jazz room of the store. As people were leaving you could feel their love for Janet, some were moved to tears.

The next time I blinked I was standing in front of Janet. I placed on the table, a beautiful postcard picture of Janet, a pine-green folder that contained my business card and an excerpt from my memoir describing Janet in concert with her brothers back in the 70's. Janet and I exchanged greetings and while she signed the postcard, I showed her the excerpt, to the chagrin of the security guard who insisted, "We're not reading anything right now." Janet leaned forward, quickly skimming the page. She picked everything up, held it to her heart and asked if she could keep it. Her eyes are big and very beautiful, engaging, lovingly inviting yet alert. Of course I said yes! Janet sweetly replied, "Thank you" and I said, "You're welcome" maintaining a blissed-out-ecstatic composure.

Outside, I met up with my friends and we excitedly shared our experiences. We exchanged email addresses and vowed to share any pictures that came out, then bid one another a farewell.

Who knows what will come of the pine-green folder? It's just an object. But the experience of finally meeting my favorite all-time performer will always live in my heart.

Janet Jackson
eyes beautiful
lovingly inviting
alert
another wonder of the world
a great woman
a great human being

A Dream Deferred, Permanently

The last time I searched for Daddy was around 1993 or 4. I was a caseworker for teens in foster care and I figured I'd have access to resources that could possibly lead me to Daddy. It never dawned on me whether he was alive or dead.

I started with the Manhattan Bureau of Vital Statisics now called the Department of Health and Hygiene which has a Vital Records division. They stated that Daddy's last employer was the Metropolitan Transit Authority and that I should call. When I called the MTA they confirmed his employment and that he had worked for a short while. That was as far as I got, no address or anything else.

Years later, around 2002, I began to have a very strong desire to find Daddy again, but I had mixed feelings about his well-being. Early 2003 I had a dream:

> *I entered a small one-bedroom apartment in a brownstone. I walked throughout the apartment which appeared neat and clean. I walked into the bedroom, where everything in the bedroom was covered in white sheets, except a t.v. that was left on. It was spring or summer and the sun shone through a window in the bedroom. I sat on the beautiful king-size bed and surveyed the room once more. No one was home.*

I needed confirmation. So, I began my search for Daddy again, just before summer 2003. I started from the drawing board—Sheltering Arms Children's Service, the foster care agency that would have my childhood history. Much to my surprise the Agency had moved to Harlem, near my job. So, on my lunch break, I visited the new offices on 125th Street and Fifth Avenue. I asked for the director of foster care. She was not available so I left my number. Within days I received a call from the director and I explained my situation. She sent a letter and A Release Of Information Form for me to complete. The letter suggested that I check the Social Security Death Index on the internet, to determine whether or not Daddy had passed away. I did feel a little uneasy and prayed there was no record of my father's death.

It appeared Daddy passed away in 1984, just two years after I graduated from college. I still hoped it was all a mistake, so I filed for the death certificate. I believe it costs $30 per request. Somewhere in my being, though, I felt Daddy was gone. I was okay especially since it was so long ago, and I became more concerned about *how* Daddy died. I never knew Daddy to attract violence to himself so I prayed that he died of an illness or accident; anything but the hand of another person.

I received Daddy's death certificate in less than two weeks. Indeed, he died in 1984, several days before Christmas. Occlusive coronary arteriosclerosis. Basically, a heart attack. Daddy was only 51. But, as crazy as it may sound, I am happy—happy that, according to the death certificate, Daddy died of "natural causes" meaning noone killed him.

I searched for Jacqueline on the internet. According to the SSDI she died in 2001. Unfortunately Sheltering Arms had no other data by which I could search for my mother; only her beautiful name—and mine is the second half of it.

Beginning of the End

I never knew the circumstances that drove my biological mother and father apart, nor did I ever learn the circumstances that drove my mother to a life of substance abuse. And I do not know where my brother is but I hear he's alive and well. Frankly, it bothers me that he hasn't sought me out, especially since he could find me more easily than I can find him. Still I love him and I'm going to find him. No drama though. Just 'Hello, what's up?' Then see what happens.

More than anything, I want all my folks—Jacqueline, Daddy and Grandma, The Johnson's, Ma and Dad—to know that I love them and that their daughter is quite alright, by the grace that was always there.

If I set my life to music
sometimes you would hear the thrashing of
brass and roll and thunder of drums, with many strings plucked and
stroked in harmony; sometimes you would hear loud, incoherent,
electrifying
piercing sounds, other times you would
see me hop, skip and jump and swing;
sometimes you would hear rhyme bouncing on the waves of a funky
beat; other times you would just hear the moan and groan of a cello
in the middle of a desert

but what makes it all sacred
is the Gospel of love.

If I compared my life to the stock market
sometimes I get everything I want and need
other times I would just
c r
  a
  s
  h
wondering
where I went wrong
but what makes it sacred is gratitude
for another chance to serve people
knowing God's abundance is infinite
and I wouldn't
trade it
for anything in the world.

If I compared my life to nature
sometimes it would be as calm
as a bird in flight
sometimes it would be as clear as a
cloudless sky
revealing its bluest eye

and other times my life would be
a natural disaster
but what makes it sacred is that I survive the 'perfect storm.'

If you saw a movie of my life
sometimes you would laugh so hard
you would keel over, fall off your chair
while holding your belly and slapping your knee and stomping your feet
and
wiping tears from your eyes;
other times you would just see a
blank screen; and sometimes

you would see me trying to direct a drama
complete with the special effects of
anger, desire, greed, lust, envy, and doubt and
bobbing on a
two-by-four
in the middle of the ocean
at midnight
with no moon
surrounded by sharks

but what makes it sacred
is I can change the script
step back
and let God direct.

If I compared my life to jewelry
we would see a Tiger's Eye, crystal, sapphires,
sometimes glass, sometimes ivory
silver, gold, pearls even platinum;

and other times plastic rings from the
bubble gum machine,
but what makes it sacred is the
Diamond of the Lord's Grace
and I wouldn't
trade it
for anything in the world.

—From *Sacred Blues, Poetry*

ABOUT THE AUTHOR

QUELYN PURDIE
Author/Educator/Entrepreneur

Quelyn is best known for over 15 years of being and working with youth and families. Her experience has inspired her to share her story, which she began to write in 1996.

As an educator, Quelyn has worked as a public school teacher and entrepreneur tutor who transformed failing students into learners of excellence and fine character. Quelyn also taught at The Bridges Juvenile Center (formerly known as Spofford Juvenile Detention) in Bronx, New York, and she served as a caseworker at an independent living program for teenagers in foster care. Quelyn wins trust and respect from her students by respecting their individual learning style and temperament.

In 2002 Quelyn created OLOWOTOT® Productions out of a desire to educate through exciting writing workshops (The Harlem Writing Salon™) and literature that speaks to family and Hip Hop themes. Her vision is to produce literature that educate and deliver images of integrity through portraying wisdom, chance, courage, intelligent humor, majesty, artistry and love.

Quelyn was a featured entrepreneur in the New York Amsterdam News in honor of Women's History Month, March 2003. She lives in Bronx, New York.

Other writings by Quelyn:

Books—Sacred Blues Poetry, Fearless Creative Writing Workbook
Screenplays—Glenda's Girls, mother.com
Journal—*For Mothers And Fathers*, a one-page journal for parenting
in today's world.

Columbia University Station
P. O. Box 250697
New York, NY 10025

0-595-32477-0

www.ingramcontent.com/pod-product-compliance
Lightning Source LLC
Chambersburg PA
CBHW031234280526
45784CB00004B/1570